BONUS! **LOOK FOR THE CAMERA** in our instructions and watch our technique videos made just for you! **www.LeisureArts.com/75546**

FAMILY FAVORITES

This handy little book has a big collection of popular gifts to crochet using medium weight yarn. Most are for Easy skill level.

LEISURE ARTS, INC. • Maumelle, Arkansas

MARY JANE SLIPPERS

EASY

SHOPPING LIST

Yarn (Medium Weight) MEDIUM 4
[4 ounces, 235 yards
(113 grams, 215 meters) per
skein]:
- ☐ Main Color (Purple) - 1 skein
- ☐ Contrasting Color (Cream) - 12{15} yards/11{13.5} meters

Crochet Hook
- ☐ Size G (4 mm)
  or size needed for gauge

Additional Supplies
- ☐ $^{7}/_{8}$" (22 mm) Buttons - 2
- ☐ Sewing needle & matching thread

SIZE INFORMATION

Finished Measurements
Child: 8" (20.5 cm) long
Adult: 10" (25.5 cm) long

Size Note: We have printed the instructions for the sizes in different colors to make it easier for you to find:
- Child size in Blue
- Adult size in Pink

Instructions in Black apply to both sizes.

GAUGE INFORMATION

15 dc and 9 rows/rnds = 4" (10 cm)
Gauge Swatch: 2½" (6.25 cm) diameter
Work same as Toe Rnds 1-3, page 4: 24 dc.

STITCH GUIDE

SINGLE CROCHET 2 TOGETHER
(abbreviated sc2tog)

Pull up a loop in each of next 2 dc, YO and draw through all 3 loops on hook **(counts as one sc)**.

REVERSE SINGLE CROCHET
(abbreviated reverse sc)

Working from **left** to **right**, ★ insert hook in st to right of hook ***(Fig. A)***, YO and draw through, under and to left of loop on hook (2 loops on hook) ***(Fig. B)***, YO and draw through both loops on hook ***(Fig. C) (reverse sc made, Fig. D)***; repeat from ★ around.

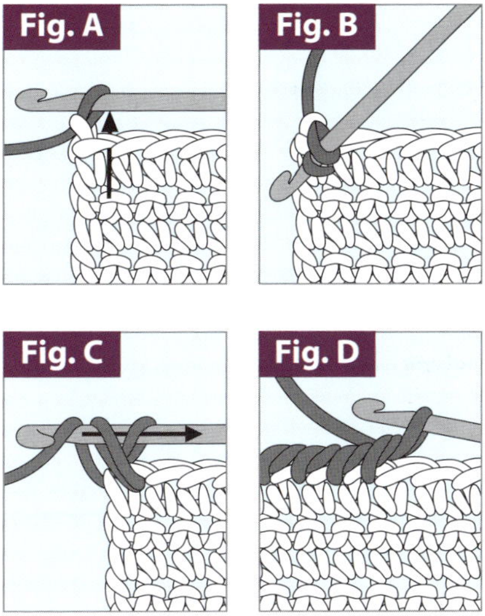

INSTRUCTIONS

TOE

Rnd 1 (Right side)**:** With Main Color, make an adjustable loop to form a ring ***(Figs. 1a-d, page 45)***, ch 2 **(beginning ch-2 does not count as a st, now and throughout)**, work 8 dc in ring; join with slip st to top of beginning ch-2.

Note: Loop a short piece of yarn around any stitch to mark Rnd 1 as **right** side.

Rnd 2: Ch 2, 2 dc in each dc around; join with slip st to top of beginning ch-2: 16 dc.

Rnd 3: Ch 2, dc in first dc, 2 dc in next dc, (dc in next dc, 2 dc in next dc) around; join with slip st to top of beginning ch-2: 24 dc.

Rnd 4: Ch 2, dc in first 2 dc, 2 dc in next dc, (dc in next 2 dc, 2 dc in next dc) around; join with slip st to top of beginning ch-2: 32 dc.

Adult Size Only

Rnd 5: Ch 2, dc in first 3 dc, 2 dc in next dc, (dc in next 3 dc, 2 dc in next dc) around; join with slip st to top of beginning ch-2: 40 dc.

Both Sizes

Rnd 5{6}: Ch 2, dc in each dc around; join with slip st to top of beginning ch-2.

FOOT

Begin working in rows.

Row 1: Ch 2, dc in first 23{31} dc, leave remaining 9 dc unworked.

Row 2: Ch 2, turn; dc in each dc across.

Repeat Row 2 until piece measures approximately 8{10}"/20.5{25.5} cm **or** until desired length, do **not** finish off.

Heel Seam: Fold last row with **right** side together, matching sts. Ch 1; working through **inside** loops of **both** stitches, slip st in each st across; finish off.

EDGING

Rnd 1: With **right** side facing, join Main Color with sc in heel seam ***(see Joining With Sc, page 45)***; 2 sc in end of each row across to Row 1, sc in end of Row 1, pull up a loop in same row and in same st on Toe as last dc on Row 1, YO and draw through all 3 loops on hook **(counts as one sc)**, place marker in sc just made, sc in next 9 dc, pull up a loop in top of beginning ch-2 on Toe and in end of Row 1 on Foot, YO and draw through all 3 loops on hook **(counts as one sc)**, place marker in sc just made, sc in end of same row, 2 sc in end of each row across; join with slip st to first sc, finish off.

Rnd 2: With **right** side facing, join Contrasting Color with sc in first sc; ★ sc in each sc across to marked sc, remove marker, sc2tog; repeat from ★ once **more**, sc in each sc across; join with slip st to first sc.

Rnd 3 - Left Slipper: Ch 1, working from **left** to **right**, work reverse sc in each sc around to within 4 sc of first sc2tog decrease; ch 25 (strap), work reverse sc in next sc and in each sc around; join with slip st to first st, finish off.

Rnd 3 - Right Slipper: Ch 1, working from **left** to **right**, work reverse sc in each sc around to 4 sc after second sc2tog decrease, ch 25 (strap), work reverse sc in next sc and in each sc around; join with slip st to first st, finish off.

Sew a button to side of each Slipper opposite strap.

Design by Marly Bird.

FAMILY CUFFED SLIPPERS

INTERMEDIATE

SHOPPING LIST

Yarn (Medium Weight) MEDIUM 4
[4 ounces, 235 yards (113 grams, 215 meters) per skein]:
☐ 1 skein

Crochet Hook
☐ Size G (4 mm) **or** size needed for gauge

SIZE INFORMATION

Finished Measurements

Small: 9" long x 7¼" circumference (23 cm x 18.5 cm)
Medium: 10" long x 8" circumference (25.5 cm x 20.5 cm)
Large: 11" long x 9¼" circumference (28 cm x 23.5 cm)
XLarge: 11½" long x 10" circumference (29 cm x 25.5 cm)

Size Note: We have printed the instructions for the sizes in different colors to make it easier for you to find:

- Size Small in Blue
- Size Medium in Pink
- Size Large in Green
- Size XLarge in Purple

Instructions in Black apply to all sizes.

GAUGE INFORMATION

12 sc and 14 rnds = 4" (10 cm)

Gauge Swatch: 2" wide (flattened) x 4" high (5 cm x 10 cm)

Ch 12; being careful **not** to twist ch, join with slip st to form a ring.

Rnd 1: Ch 1, sc in each ch around; place marker to indicate beginning of rnd ***(see Markers, page 45)***: 12 sc.

Rnds 2-14: Sc in each sc around.

Finish off.

STITCH GUIDE

SINGLE CROCHET 2 TOGETHER ***(abbreviated sc2tog)***
Pull up a loop in each of next 2 sc, YO and draw through all 3 loops on hook (**counts as one sc**).

This slipper is worked from the top down, beginning at the ankle, with a turned heel and round toe. The Cuff is added after completing the Toe.

INSTRUCTIONS

ANKLE

Ch 22{24-28-30} **loosely**; being careful **not** to twist ch, join with slip st to form a ring.

Rnd 1 (Right side)**:** Ch 1, sc in each ch around; place marker to indicate beginning of rnd ***(see Markers, page 45)***: 22{24-28-30} sc.

Rnds 2 thru 4{5-6-6}: Sc in each sc around.

HEEL

Begin working in rows.

Row 1: Sc in next 10{12-14-14} sc, leave remaining sc unworked.

Row 2: Ch 1, turn; sc in each sc across.

Row 3 (Decrease row)**:** Ch 1, turn; sc in each sc across to last sc, leave last sc unworked: 9{11-13-13} sc.

Repeat Row 3, 3{5-7-7} times: 6 sc.

TURNING HEEL

Row 1: Ch 1, turn; sc in each sc across, sc in next skipped sc 2 rows **below**, slip st in end of row **below** last sc made: 7 sc.

Row 2: Turn; skip first slip st, sc in each sc across, sc in next skipped sc 2 rows **below**, slip st in end of row **below** last sc made: 8 sc.

Repeat Row 2, 2{4-6-6} times: 10{12-14-14} sc.

FOOT

Resume working in rounds.

Rnd 1 (Right side)**:** Turn; skip first slip st, sc in each sc around: 22{24-28-30} sc.

Continuing with **right** side facing, sc in each sc around until Foot measures $8\frac{1}{2}${$9\frac{1}{2}$-$10\frac{1}{2}$-11}"/ 21.5{24-26.5-28} cm from center of Heel.

TOE

★ Sc in next 4 sc, sc2tog; repeat from ★ 5{5-11-9} times **more**: 16{18-16-20} sc.

Flatten slipper centering Heel; place a marker in st at each fold.

If necessary, sc in each sc across to marker at first fold.

Top Seam: Turn Slipper inside out and fold last row flat at markers. Working through **inside** loops of **both** stitches, slip st in each st across; finish off.

CUFF

Rnd 1: With **right** side facing and working in free loops of beginning ch ***(Fig. 5, page 46)***, join yarn with sc in any ch ***(see Joining With Sc, page 45)***; sc in each ch around, place marker to indicate beginning of rnd.

Rnds 2-10: Sc in each sc around.

Slip st in next sc, finish off.

Fold Cuff to outside.

Design by Darla Sims.

BABY BOOTIES & MITTS

EASY

Size: 6 Months
Booties: 4¹/₄" (10.75 cm) long
Mitts: 4¹/₂" long x 6³/₄" circumference (11.5 cm x 17 cm)

SHOPPING LIST

Yarn (Medium Weight) MEDIUM 4
[4 ounces, 235 yards
(113 grams, 215 meters) per
skein]:
☐ Color A (Light Blue) -
80 yards (73 meters)
☐ Color B (White) -
60 yards (55 meters)

Crochet Hook
☐ Size G (4 mm)
or size needed for gauge

Additional Supplies
☐ Yarn needle

GAUGE INFORMATION

7 sc and 8 rows/rnds = 2" (5 cm)
Gauge Swatch: 2" (5 cm) square
With Color A, ch 8.
Row 1: Sc in second ch from hook and in each ch across: 7 sc.
Rows 2-8: Ch 1, turn; sc in each sc across.
Finish off.

STITCH GUIDE

SINGLE CROCHET 2 TOGETHER
(abbreviated sc2tog)

Pull up a loop in each of next 2 sts, YO and draw through all 3 loops on hook (**counts as one sc**).

HALF DOUBLE CROCHET 2 TOGETHER
(abbreviated hdc2tog)
(uses next 2 sts)

★ YO, insert hook in **next** st, YO and pull up a loop; repeat from ★ once **more**, YO and draw through all 5 loops on hook (**counts as one hdc**).

BOOTIE (Make 2)

SOLE

With Color A, ch 13.

Rnd 1 (Right side)**:** Sc in second ch from hook and in next 8 chs, hdc in next ch, 2 hdc in next ch, 3 hdc in last ch; working in free loops of beginning ch ***(Fig. 5, page 46)***, 2 hdc in next ch, hdc in next ch, sc in next 8 chs, 2 sc in next ch; do **not** join, place marker to indicate beginning of rnd ***(see Markers, page 45)***: 28 sts.

Rnd 2: 2 Sc in next st, sc in next 10 sts, 2 sc in next st, (sc in next st, 2 sc in next st) twice, sc in next 11 sts, 2 sc in next st: 33 sc.

Rnd 3: 2 Sc in next sc, sc in next 11 sc, 2 sc in next sc, (sc in next sc, 2 sc in next sc) 3 times, sc in next 13 sc, 2 sc in next sc: 39 sc.

SIDES

Rnd 1: Sc in Back Loop Only of each sc around ***(Fig. 3, page 46)***, changing to Color B in sc at end of rnd ***(Fig. 6a, page 46)***; cut Color A.

Rnd 2: Sc in both loops of each sc around.

Rnd 3: Sc in next 14 sc, sc2tog, (sc in next sc, sc2tog) 3 times, sc in next 14 sc: 35 sc.

Rnd 4: Sc in next 13 sc, sc2tog 5 times, sc in next 12 sc: 30 sc.

Rnd 5: Sc in next 12 sc, hdc in next 2 sc, hdc2tog, hdc in next 2 sc, sc in next 12 sc: 29 sts.

SHAPING

Begin working in rows.

Row 1: Sc in next 11 sc, hdc in next 2 sts, hdc2tog, hdc in next 2 hdc, sc in next sc, slip st in next sc, leave remaining sts unworked; do **not** remove marker: 18 sts.

Row 2: Ch 1, turn; skip first slip st, sc in next sc, hdc2tog twice, sc in next hdc, slip st in next sc, leave remaining sts unworked: 5 sts.

Resume working in rounds.

Rnd 1: Ch 1, turn; skip first slip st, hdc2tog twice, sc in end of next row and in next 10 sc on Sides (to marker).

Rnd 2: Sc in next 10 sc, sc in end of next row, sc in next 2 hdc and in next 11 sc: 24 sc.

CUFF

Begin working in rows.

Row 1: Hdc in first 12 sc, leave remaining 12 sc unworked, remove marker.

Row 2: Ch 1, turn; hdc in all 24 sts.

Rows 3 and 4: Ch 1, turn; hdc in each hdc across.

Row 5: Ch 1, turn; hdc in first 12 hdc, cut Color B, with Color A, slip st in next st ***(Fig. 6b, page 46)***, leave remaining sts unworked.

Edging: Ch 1, turn; sc in each hdc and in end of each row around; join with slip st to first sc, finish off.

MITT (Make 2)

RIBBING

With Color A, ch 7.

Row 1 (Right side)**:** Sc in back ridge ***(Fig. 2, page 46)*** of second ch from hook and in each ch across: 6 sc.

Note: Loop a short piece of yarn around any stitch to mark Row 1 as **right** side.

Rows 2-20: Ch 1, turn; sc in Back Loop Only of each sc across ***(Fig. 3, page 46)***.

Joining Row: Ch 1, turn; hold beginning ch and last row with **right** side together, working in Back Loops Only of **each** layer, slip st in each st across; do **not** finish off.

BODY

Begin working in rounds.

Rnd 1 (Right side)**:** Sc in end of each row across Ribbing; do **not** join, place marker to indicate beginning of rnd *(see Markers, page 45)*: 20 sc.

Rnd 2: (Sc in next 4 sc, 2 sc in next sc) 4 times: 24 sc.

Rnds 3-6: Sc in each sc around.

Rnd 7: Sc in each sc around changing to Color B in sc at end of rnd *(Fig. 6a, page 46)*; cut Color A.

Rnds 8-10: Sc in each sc around.

SHAPING

Rnd 1: (Sc2tog, sc in next sc) 8 times: 16 sc.

Rnd 2: Sc in next sc, (sc2tog, sc in next sc) 5 times: 11 sc.

Rnd 3: Sc2tog 5 times, sc in next sc; slip st in next sc, finish off leaving a long end for sewing: 6 sc.

Thread yarn needle with long end and weave needle through sts on Rnd 3 *(Fig. 8, page 47)*; pull tightly to close and secure end.

Designs by Candi Jensen.

FAMILY HAT

EASY

SHOPPING LIST

Yarn (Medium Weight) MEDIUM 4

[4 ounces, 235 yards (113 grams, 215 meters) per skein]:

- ☐ Main Color - 1 skein
- ☐ Contrasting Color - 1 skein

Crochet Hook

- ☐ Size H (5 mm) **or** size needed for gauge

Additional Supplies

- ☐ Yarn needle

SIZE INFORMATION

Finished Measurements

Small: 17¼" (44 cm) circumference

Medium: 19¼" (49 cm) circumference

Large: 21¼" (54 cm) circumference

Size Note: We have printed the instructions for the sizes in different colors to make it easier for you to find:

- Size Small in Blue
- Size Medium in Pink
- Size Large in Green

Instructions in Black apply to all sizes.

GAUGE INFORMATION

In Ribbing,16 sts and 14 rows = 4½" (11.5 cm)

In Body pattern,16 sts and 12 rows = 4½" (11.5 cm)

Gauge Swatch: 4½" (11.5 cm) square

Work same as Ribbing, page 15, for 14 rows: 16 sc.

STITCH GUIDE

SINGLE CROCHET 2 TOGETHER
(abbreviated sc2tog)
Pull up a loop in each of next 2 dc, YO and draw through all 3 loops on hook (**counts as one sc**).

DOUBLE CROCHET 2 TOGETHER
(abbreviated dc2tog)
(uses next 2 sts)
★ YO, insert hook in **next** st, YO and pull up a loop, YO and draw through 2 loops on hook; repeat from ★ once **more**, YO and draw through all 3 loops on hook (**counts as one dc**).

INSTRUCTIONS

RIBBING

With Main Color, ch 17.

Row 1 (Right side)**:** Sc in back ridge ***(Fig. 2, page 46)*** of second ch from hook and each ch across: 16 sc.

Note: Loop a short piece of yarn around any stitch to mark Row 1 as **right** side.

Rows 2 thru 54{60-66}: Ch 1, turn; sc in Back Loop Only ***(Fig. 3, page 46)*** of each sc across.

Joining Row: Ch 1, turn; hold beginning ch and last row with **right** side together, working in Back Loops Only of **each** layer, slip st in each st across; do **not** finish off.

BODY

Rnd 1: Ch 1, with **wrong** side of Ribbing facing (right side of hat after Ribbing is turned up for cuff), sc in end of each row around; join with slip st to first sc: 54{60-66} sc.

Rnd 2: Ch 3 **(counts as first dc, now and throughout)**, dc in next sc and in each sc around; drop Main Color, with Contrasting Color, join with slip st to first dc ***(Fig. 6b, page 46)***.

Do **not** cut yarn until instructed; carry unused yarn loosely along **wrong** side.

Rnd 3: Ch 1, sc in same st as joining and in each dc around; drop Contrasting Color, with Main Color, join with slip st to first sc.

Rnd 4: Ch 3, dc in next sc and in each sc around; drop Main Color, with Contrasting Color, join with slip st to first dc.

Repeat Rnds 3 and 4 for pattern until Body measures approximately 5 1/2{6-6 1/2}"/ 14{15-16.5} cm from top of ribbing, ending by working Rnd 3.

SHAPING

Size Small ONLY

Rnd 1: Ch 3, dc in next 3 sc, dc2tog, (dc in next 4 sc, dc2tog) around; drop Main Color, with Contrasting Color, join with slip st to first dc: 45 dc.

Size Medium ONLY

Rnd 1: Ch 3, dc in next sc, dc2tog, (dc in next 2 sc, dc2tog) around; drop Main Color, with Contrasting Color, join with slip st to first dc: 45 dc.

Size Large ONLY

Rnd 1: Ch 3, (dc in next sc, dc2tog) around to last 2 sc, dc in last 2 sc; drop Main Color, with Contrasting Color, join with slip st to first dc: 45 dc.

All Sizes

Rnd 2: Ch 1, sc in same st as joining, sc2tog, (sc in next dc, sc2tog) around; cut Contrasting Color, with Main Color, join with slip st to first dc: 30 sc.

Rnd 3: Ch 2, dc in next sc, dc2tog around; skip beginning ch-2 and join with slip st to first dc: 15 dc.

Rnd 4: Ch 2, dc2tog around; skip beginning ch-2 and join with slip st to first dc, finish off leaving a long end for sewing: 7 dc.

Thread yarn needle with long end and weave needle through sts on Rnd 4 ***(Fig. 8, page 47)***; pull tightly to close and secure end.

Turn Cuff to right side.

Design by Becky Stevens.

FAMILY NECKWEAR

EASY +

SHOPPING LIST

Yarn (Medium Weight) MEDIUM 4
[4 ounces, 235 yards (113 grams, 215 meters) per skein]:

Solid Scarf

- ☐ Main Color - 1 skein

2-Color Scarf

- ☐ Main Color (Red) - 1 skein
- ☐ Contrasting Color (Blue) - 1 skein

Hooded Scarf

- ☐ Main Color - 2 skeins
- ☐ Contrasting Color - 1 skein

Cowl

- ☐ 1 skein

Crochet Hook

- ☐ Size I (5.5 mm) **or** size needed for gauge

Additional Supplies

- ☐ Yarn needle

SIZE INFORMATION

Finished Measurements

Note: Either scarf can be striped.

Long Scarf: 5" wide x 54½" long (12.5 cm x 138.5 cm)

Short Scarf: 7" wide x 45½" long (18 cm x 115.5 cm)

Hooded Scarf: 17½" (44.5 cm) hood width

Cowl: 12½" wide x 27" circumference (32 cm x 68.5 cm)

Size Note: We have printed the instructions for the Scarf sizes in different colors to make it easier for you to find:

- Long Scarf in Blue
- Short Scarf in Green

Instructions in Black apply to both sizes.

GAUGE INFORMATION

In pattern, (ex sc, ch 1) 4 times and 4 rows = 2" (5 cm)

Gauge Swatches:

Long Scarf & Cowl: $4^{1}/_{2}$" wide x 4" high (11.5 cm x 10 cm)

With Main Color, ch 20. Work same as Scarf for 8 rows: 9 ex sc and 9 sps. Finish off for Cowl only.

Short Scarf & Hooded Scarf: $6^{1}/_{2}$" wide x 4" high (16.5 cm x 10 cm)

With Main Color, ch 28. Work same as Scarf for 8 rows: 13 ex sc and 13 sps.

STITCH GUIDE

EXTENDED SINGLE CROCHET *(abbreviated ex sc)*

Insert hook in st or sp indicated, YO and pull a loop, YO and draw through one loop on hook, YO and draw through both loops on hook.

OPTIONAL STRIPE SEQUENCE

Work Rows 1 and 2 with Main Color, changing to Contrasting Color in last ex sc at end of Row 2 *(Fig. 6a, page 46)*; cut yarn. Work 2 rows with Contrasting Color, 4 rows with Main Color, 4 rows with Contrasting Color, 12 rows with Main Color, ★ 6 rows with Contrasting Color, 12 rows with Main Color; repeat from ★ 3{2} times **more**, 4 rows with Contrasting Color, 4 rows with Main Color, 2 rows with Contrasting Color, 2 rows with Main Color.

SCARF

With Main Color, ch 20{28}.

Row 1 (Right side)**:** Ex sc in fourth ch from hook **(3 skipped chs count as first sp)**, ★ ch 1, skip next ch, ex sc in next ch; repeat from ★ across: 9{13} ex sc and 9{13} sps.

Note: Loop a short piece of yarn around any stitch to mark Row 1 as **right** side.

Row 2: Ch 3 **(counts as first sp)**, turn; ex sc in first ch-1 sp, ch 1, ★ skip next ex sc, ex sc in next ch-1 sp, ch 1; repeat from ★ across to last ex sc, skip last ex sc, ex sc in last sp.

Repeat Row 2 for pattern until piece measures approximately 54{45}"/137{114.5} cm from beginning ch **or** until Optional Stripe Sequence is complete, ending by working a **wrong** side row; do **not** finish off.

Edging: Ch 1, turn; sc evenly around entire Scarf working 3 sc in each corner; join with slip st to first sc, finish off.

HOODED SCARF

FIRST SIDE

With Main Color, ch 28.

Row 1 (Right side)**:** Ex sc in fourth ch from hook **(3 skipped chs count as first sp)**, ★ ch 1, skip next ch, ex sc in next ch; repeat from ★ across: 13 ex sc and 13 sps.

Note: Loop a short piece of yarn around any stitch to mark Row 1 as **right** side.

Row 2: Ch 3 **(counts as first sp)**, turn; ex sc in first ch-1 sp, ch 1, ★ skip next ex sc, ex sc in next ch-1 sp, ch 1; repeat from ★ across to last ex sc, skip last ex sc, ex sc in last sp.

Repeat Row 2 for pattern until First Side measures approximately 20" (51 cm) from beginning ch, ending by working a **wrong** side row: 13 ex sc and 13 sps.

HOOD

Row 1: Ch 10; ex sc in fourth ch from hook, ch 1, (skip next ch, ex sc in next ch, ch 1) 3 times, ★ skip next ex sc, ex sc in next ch-1 sp, ch 1; repeat from ★ across to last ex sc, skip last ex sc, ex sc in last sp: 17 ex sc and 17 sps.

Work in pattern until Hood measures approximately 17" (43 cm) from beginning ch of Hood, ending by working a **right** side row.

SECOND SIDE

Row 1: Ch 3, turn; ex sc in first ch-1 sp, ★ ch 1, skip next ex sc, ex sc in next ch-1 sp; repeat from ★ 11 times **more**, leave remaining ex sc unworked: 13 ex sc and 13 sps.

Work in pattern until Second Side measures same as First Side, ending by working a **right** side row.

Finish off.

Fold Hood in half with **right** side together; using Main Color, whipstitch across end of rows *(Fig. 7b, page 47)*.

Edging: With **right** side facing, join Contrasting Color with sc in first st on Second Side *(see Joining With Sc, page 45)*; sc evenly around working 3 sc in each corner of Scarf; join with slip st to first sc, finish off.

COWL

Ch 50.

Row 1 (Right side)**:** Ex sc in fourth ch from hook **(3 skipped chs count as first sp)**, ★ ch 1, skip next ch, ex sc in next ch; repeat from ★ across: 24 ex sc and 24 sps.

Note: Loop a short piece of yarn around any stitch to mark Row 1 as **right** side.

Row 2: Ch 3 **(counts as first sp)**, turn; ex sc in first ch-1 sp, ch 1, ★ skip next ex sc, ex sc in next ch-1 sp, ch 1; repeat from ★ across to last ex sc, skip last ex sc, ex sc in last sp.

Repeat Row 2 for pattern until Cowl measures approximately 27" (68.5 cm) from beginning ch, ending by working a **wrong** side row.

Finish off leaving a long end for sewing.

Thread yarn needle with long end. Holding beginning ch and last row with **right** side together, whipstitch sts together *(Fig. 7a, page 47)*.

Edging: With **right** side facing, join yarn with sc at seam ***(see Joining With Sc, page 45)***; sc evenly around end of rows; join with slip st to first sc, finish off.

Repeat Edging on opposite edge.

Designs by Becky Stevens.

LACY MITTS

EASY

SHOPPING LIST

Yarn (Medium Weight) MEDIUM 4
[4 ounces, 235 yards
(113 grams, 215 meters) per
skein]:

2-Color Mitts

- ☐ Main Color (Black) - 45{50} yards/41{45.5} meters
- ☐ Contrasting Color (Cream) - 25{42} yards/23{38.5} meters

5-Color Mitts

- ☐ Main Color (Green) - 25{35} yards/23{32} meters
- ☐ Color A (Red) - 12{14} yards/ 11{13} meters
- ☐ Color B (Orange) - 12{14} yards/11{13} meters
- ☐ Color C (Yellow) - 12{14} yards/11{13} meters
- ☐ Color D (White) - 12{14} yards/11{13} meters

Crochet Hook

- ☐ Size H (5 mm) **or** size needed for gauge

Additional Supplies

- ☐ Yarn needle

SIZE INFORMATION

Finished Measurements

Small:

6" long x 6" circumference
(15 cm x 15 cm)

Medium:

7¼" long x 7¼" circumference
(18.5 cm x 18.5 cm)

Size Note: We have printed the instructions for the sizes in different colors to make it easier for you to find:

- Size Small in Blue
- Size Medium in Pink

Instructions in Black apply to both sizes.

GAUGE INFORMATION

In pattern,

(sc, ch 3, work Cluster, ch 1) 3 times = 3½" (9 cm), 8 rows = 4½" (11.5 cm)

Gauge Swatch: 6{7¼}" wide x 2¼" high **[**15.25{18.5} cm x 5.75 cm**]**
Work same as Mitt, page 27, through Row 4: 6{7} Clusters, 5{6} sps, and 5{6} sc.

STITCH GUIDE

BEGINNING CLUSTER (uses 2 chs)
Ch 4, turn; YO, insert hook in third ch from hook, YO and pull up a loop, YO and draw through 2 loops on hook, YO, insert hook in last ch, YO and pull up a loop, YO and draw through 2 loops on hook, YO and draw through all 3 loops on hook.

CLUSTER (uses one st or sp)
★ YO, insert hook in st or sp indicated, YO and pull up a loop, YO and draw through 2 loops on hook; repeat from ★ once **more**, YO and draw through all 3 loops on hook.

ENDING CLUSTER (uses last sp and last sc)
★ YO, insert hook in last sp (same sp as sc just made), YO and pull up a loop, YO and draw through 2 loops on hook; repeat from ★ once **more**, insert hook in last sc, YO and pull up a loop, YO and draw through all 4 loops on hook.

Note: When changing colors at end of row, work Ending Cluster to last step (4 loops on hook), cut yarn; with next color, YO and draw through all 4 loops on hook.

STRIPE SEQUENCE

Note: When changing colors ***(Fig. 6a, page 46)***, cut yarn leaving a long end for sewing.

2-COLOR STRIPE SEQUENCE

Two rows **each**: ★ Main Color, Contrasting Color; repeat from ★ 1{2} time(s) **more**; then work 3{1} row(s) with Main Color.

5-COLOR STRIPE SEQUENCE

One row **each**: ★ Main Color, Color A, Color B, Color C, Color D; repeat from ★ once **more**; then work 1{3} row(s) with Main Color.

INSTRUCTIONS

With Main Color, ch 22{26}.

Work in desired Stripe Sequence changing colors in last stitch made on previous row.

Row 1 (Right side)**:** (Sc, ch 3, work Cluster) in second ch from hook, ch 1, ★ skip next 3 chs, (sc, ch 3, work Cluster) in next ch, ch 1; repeat from ★ across to last 4 chs, skip next 3 chs, sc in last ch: 5{6} Clusters, 5{6} ch-3 sps, and 6{7} sc.

Note: Loop a short piece of yarn around any stitch to mark Row 1 as **right** side.

Row 2: Work Beginning Cluster, ch 1, ★ (sc, ch 3, work Cluster) in next ch-3 sp, ch 1; repeat from ★ 3{4} times **more**, sc in last sp, ch 2, work Ending Cluster: 6{7} Clusters, 4{5} ch-3 sps, and 5{6} sc.

Row 3: Ch 1, turn; sc in top of Ending Cluster, ch 2, work Cluster in next ch-2 sp, ch 1, ★ (sc, ch 3, work Cluster) in next ch-3 sp, ch 1; repeat from ★ across, sc in top of Beginning Cluster: 5{6} Clusters, 4{5} ch-3 sps, and 6{7} sc.

Rows 4 thru 11{13}: Repeat Rows 2 and 3, 4{5} times.

Finish off leaving a long end for sewing.

Fold Mitt in half with **right** side together matching end of rows. Using matching colors, sew Row 1 through Row 3 together. Skip next 3 rows for thumb opening and sew remaining rows together.

Repeat for second Mitt.

Design by Marly Bird.

BASIC MITTS

EASY

SHOPPING LIST

Yarn (Medium Weight) MEDIUM 4
[4 ounces, 235 yards
(113 grams, 215 meters) per skein]:
☐ 1 skein

Crochet Hook
☐ Size H (5 mm)
or size needed for gauge

Additional Supplies
☐ Yarn needle

SIZE INFORMATION

The Mitts are worked across the length and can be worked to any circumference or as suggested.

Finished Measurements

Small: 5" long x 6" circumference (12.75 cm x 15 cm)
Medium: 6" long x 7" circumference (15 cm x 18 cm)
Large: 7" long x 8" circumference (18 cm x 20.5 cm)
XLarge: 8" long x 9" circumference (20.5 cm x 23 cm)

Size Note: We have printed the instructions for the sizes in different colors to make it easier for you to find:

- Size Small in Blue
- Size Medium in Pink
- Size Large in Green
- Size XLarge in Purple

Instructions in Black apply to all sizes.

GAUGE INFORMATION

In pattern, 12 sts = 4" (10 cm)
Gauge Swatch: 5" wide x 4" high (12.75 cm x 10 cm)
Work same as size Small, page 29, through Row 4: 15 sts.
If you are making size Small, continue working; otherwise finish off.

INSTRUCTIONS

Leaving a long end for sewing, ch 16{19-22-25}.

Row 1 (Right side)**:** Sc in second ch from hook and in each ch across: 15{18-21-24} sc.

Note: Loop a short piece of yarn around any stitch to mark Row 1 as **right** side.

Row 2: Ch 2 **(does not count as first hdc)**, turn; hdc in each sc across.

Row 3: Ch 1, turn; sc in each hdc across (do **not** work in turning ch).

Repeat Rows 2 and 3 for pattern until Mitt measures approximately 6{7-8-9}"/15{18-20.5-23} cm from beginning ch **or** to desired circumference, ending by working Row 2.

Finish off leaving a long end for sewing.

Fold Mitt in half holding beginning ch and last row with **right** side together. Using long end, whipstitch sts together ***(Fig. 7a, page 47)*** for approximately 1{1½-2-2}"/ 2.5{4-5-5} cm; secure end.

Using end from the beginning ch, whipstitch sts together leaving approximately 1¼{1½-1½-2}"/ 3{4-4-5} cm free for thumb; secure end.

Repeat for second Mitt.

PET BED

EASY

SHOPPING LIST

Yarn (Medium Weight) MEDIUM 4
[4 ounces, 235 yards
(113 grams, 215 meters) per skein]:

- ☐ Main Color (Navy) - 2 skeins
- ☐ Contrasting Color (Grey) - 1 skein

Crochet Hook

- ☐ Size H (5 mm)
  or size needed for gauge

SIZE INFORMATION

Size: Small{Medium-Large}
Finished Measurements:
10{12-14}" diameter x 3½" high
[25.5{30.5-35.5} cm x 9 cm]

Size Note: We have printed the instructions for the sizes in different colors to make it easier for you to find:

- Size Small in Blue
- Size Medium in Pink
- Size Large in Green

Instructions in Black apply to all sizes.

GAUGE INFORMATION

Holding 2 strands together,
13 sc and 12 rows/rnds = 4" (10 cm)

Gauge Swatch: 4" (10 cm) square
Holding 2 strands of Main Color together, ch 14.

Row 1: Sc in second ch from hook and in each ch across: 13 sc.

Rows 2-12: Ch 1, turn; sc in each sc across.

Finish off.

STITCH GUIDE

BACK POST SINGLE CROCHET *(abbreviated BPsc)*

Insert hook from **back** to **front** around post of st indicated ***(Fig. A)***, YO and pull up a loop, YO and draw through both loops on hook.

Fig. A

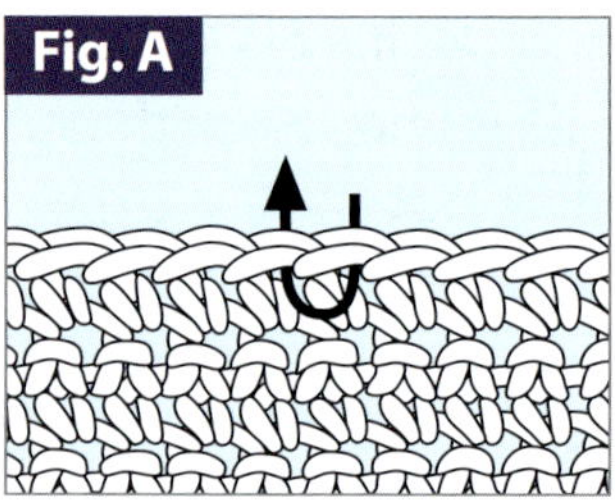

LONG SINGLE CROCHET *(abbreviated Long sc)*

Working **around** previous rnd, insert hook in sc indicated ***(Fig. B)***, YO and pull up a loop even with last st made, YO and draw through both loops on hook.

Fig. B

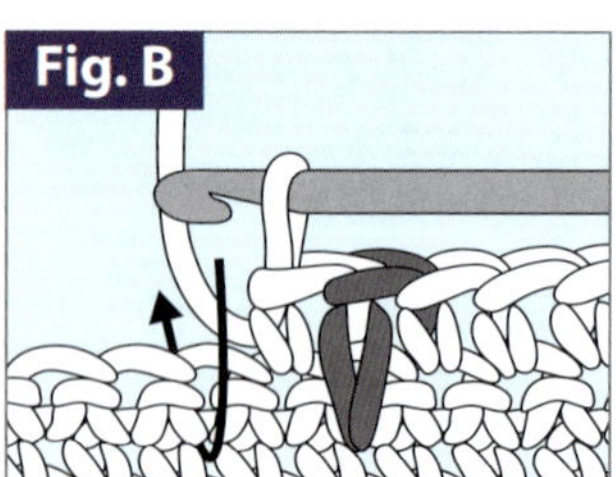

INSTRUCTIONS

Pet Bed is worked holding two strands of yarn together throughout.

BOTTOM

Rnd 1: Holding 2 strands of Main Color together, make an adjustable loop to form a ring ***(Figs. 1a-d, page 45)***, work 10 sc in ring; join with slip st to first sc.

Rnd 2: Ch 1, 2 sc in each sc around; join with slip st to first sc: 20 sc.

Rnd 3: Ch 1, 2 sc in first sc, sc in next sc, (2 sc in next sc, sc in next sc) around; join with slip st to first sc: 30 sc.

Rnd 4: Ch 1, sc in each sc around; join with slip st to first sc.

Rnd 5: Ch 1, sc in first 2 sc, 2 sc in next sc, (sc in next 2 sc, 2 sc in next sc) around; join with slip st to first sc: 40 sc.

Rnd 6: Ch 1, 2 sc in first sc, sc in next 3 sc, (2 sc in next sc, sc in next 3 sc) around; join with slip st to first sc: 50 sc.

Rnd 7: Ch 1, sc in each sc around; join with slip st to first sc.

Rnd 8: Ch 1, sc in first 4 sc, 2 sc in next sc, (sc in next 4 sc, 2 sc in next sc) around; join with slip st to first sc: 60 sc.

Rnd 9: Ch 1, 2 sc in first sc, sc in next 5 sc, (2 sc in next sc, sc in next 5 sc) around; join with slip st to first sc: 70 sc.

Rnd 10: Ch 1, sc in each sc around; join with slip st to first sc.

Rnd 11: Ch 1, sc in first 6 sc, 2 sc in next sc, (sc in next 6 sc, 2 sc in next sc) around; join with slip st to first sc: 80 sc.

Rnd 12: Ch 1, 2 sc in first sc, sc in next 7 sc, (2 sc in next sc, sc in next 7 sc) around; join with slip st to first sc: 90 sc.

Rnd 13: Ch 1, sc in each sc around; join with slip st to first sc.

Rnd 14: Ch 1, sc in first 8 sc, 2 sc in next sc, (sc in next 8 sc, 2 sc in next sc) around; join with slip st to first sc, do **not** finish off: 100 sc.

Size Medium & Size Large Only

Rnd 15: Ch 1, 2 sc in first sc, sc in next 9 sc, (2 sc in next sc, sc in next 9 sc) around; join with slip st to first sc: 110 sc.

Rnd 16: Ch 1, sc in each sc around; join with slip st to first sc.

Rnd 17: Ch 1, sc in first 10 sc, 2 sc in next sc, (sc in next 10 sc, 2 sc in next sc) around; join with slip st to first sc; do **not** finish off: 120 sc.

Size Large Only

Rnd 18: Ch 1, 2 sc in first sc, sc in next 11 sc, (2 sc in next sc, sc in next 11 sc) around; join with slip st to first sc: 130 sc.

Rnd 19: Ch 1, sc in each sc around; join with slip st to first sc.

Rnd 20: Ch 1, sc in first 12 sc, 2 sc in next sc, (sc in next 12 sc, 2 sc in next sc) around; join with slip st to first sc, do **not** finish off: 140 sc.

SIDES - All Sizes

Rnd 1 (Right side)**:** Ch 1, **turn**; work BPsc around next sc and each sc around; join with slip st to first BPsc: 100{120-140} BPsc.

Rnds 2-4: Ch 1, do **not** turn; sc in each st around; join with slip st to first sc.

Rnd 5: Ch 1, sc in each sc around; cut Main Color, holding 2 strands of Contrasting Color together, join with slip st to first sc *(Fig. 6b, page 46)*.

Rnd 6: Ch 1, sc in first 4 sc, work Long sc in sc one rnd **below** next sc, ★ sc in next 4 sc, work Long sc in sc one rnd **below** next sc; repeat from ★ around; join with slip st to first sc: 20{24-28} Long sc and 80{96-112} sc.

Rnds 7-9: Ch 1, sc in each st around; join with slip st to first sc.

Rnd 10: Ch 1, (slip st in next sc, ch 1) around; join with slip st to joining slip st, finish off.

Design by Marly Bird.

BARGELLO COVER-UPS

Everyone in the family can enjoy one of these four sizes.

INTERMEDIATE

SHOPPING LIST

Yarn (Medium Weight) MEDIUM 4
[4 ounces, 235 yards (113 grams, 215 meters) per skein]:

- ☐ Color A - 1{3-3-6} skeins
- ☐ Color B - 1{3-3-5} skeins
- ☐ Color C - 1{3-3-5} skeins

Note: See Yarn Information on page 48 for specific colors used. Car Seat Cover is shown on page 37 and Lap Robe is shown on page 39. Baby Blanket and afghan sizes are not shown.

Crochet Hook

- ☐ Size I (5.5 mm) **or** size needed for gauge

SIZE INFORMATION

Finish Measurements

Car Seat Cover: 15½" x 21" (39.5 cm x 53.5 cm)
Baby Blanket: 34½" x 45" (87.5 cm x 114.5 cm)
Lap Robe: 36" x 50½" (91.5 cm x 128.5 cm)
Afghan: 47½" x 63¾" (120.5 cm x 162 cm)

Size Note: We have printed the instructions for the sizes in different colors to make it easier for you to find:

- Car Seat Cover in Blue
- Baby Blanket in Pink
- Lap Robe in Green
- Afghan in Purple

Instructions in Black apply to all sizes.

GAUGE INFORMATION

In pattern,
15 sts = 4" (10 cm),
12 rows = $3\frac{3}{4}$" (9.5 cm)

Gauge Swatch: 5" wide x $3\frac{3}{4}$" high (12.75 cm x 9.5 cm)
With Color A, ch 20.
Work same as Body Rows 1-12: 10 sts and 3 ch-3 sps.
Finish off.

STRIPE SEQUENCE

Work 5 rows with Color A, ★ work 2 rows **each**: Color B, Color C, Color A; repeat from ★ for Stripe Sequence.

INSTRUCTIONS

BODY

Each row is worked across length of Cover-Up.

With Color A, ch 80{170-190-240}.

Row 1 (Right side)**:** Sc in second ch from hook and in each ch across: 79{169-189-239} sc.

Note: Loop a short piece of yarn around any stitch to mark Row 1 as **right** side.

Row 2: Ch 1, turn; sc in first 3 sc, ch 3, ★ skip next 3 sc, sc in next 2 sc, ch 3; repeat from ★ across to last 6 sc, skip next 3 sc, sc in last 3 sc: 34{70-78-98} sc and 15{33-37-47} ch-3 sps.

Row 3: Ch 1, turn; sc in first sc, ch 2, ★ skip next 2 sc, working in **front** of next ch-3 ***(Fig. 4, page 46)***, dc in 3 skipped sc on row **below** ch-3, ch 2; repeat from ★ across to last 3 sc, skip next 2 sc, sc in last sc: 47{101-113-143} sts and 16{34-38-48} ch-2 sps.

Row 4: Ch 1, turn; sc in first sc, working **behind** next ch-2, dc in 2 skipped sts on row **below** ch-2, ★ ch 3, skip next 3 dc, working **behind** next ch-2, dc in 2 skipped sts on row **below** ch-2; repeat from ★ across to last sc, sc in last sc: 34{70-78-98} sc and 15{33-37-47} ch-3 sps.

WARNING
ADVERTENCIA

Row 5: Ch 1, turn; sc in first sc, ch 2, ★ skip next 2 dc, working in **front** of next ch-3, dc in 3 skipped dc on row **below** ch-3, ch 2; repeat from ★ across to last 3 sts, skip next 2 dc, sc in last sc changing to next color in Stripe Sequence *(Fig. 6a, page 46)*; cut yarn: 47{101-113-143} sts and 16{34-38-48} ch-2 sps.

Repeat Rows 4 and 5 for pattern until Body measures approximately 14½{33½-35-46½}"/ 37{85-89-118} cm from beginning ch, ending by working Row 5 with Color A; do **not** change colors.

Next Row: With Color A, repeat Row 4.

Last Row: Ch 1, turn; sc in first sc, ★ sc in next 2 dc, working in **front** of next ch-3, dc in next 3 skipped dc on row **below** ch-3; repeat from ★ across to last 3 sts, sc in last 3 sts; finish off.

EDGING

FIRST SIDE

With **right** side facing, join Color A with slip st in first sc on Last Row; ★ ch 1, skip next st, slip st in next st; repeat from ★ across; finish off.

SECOND SIDE

With **right** side facing and working in free loops of beginning ch *(Fig. 5, page 46)*, join Color A with slip st in first ch; ★ ch 1, skip next ch, slip st in next ch; repeat from ★ across; finish off.

Design by Anne Halliday.

BASKET

EASY

Finished Size: 10" diameter x 10½" high (at side) (25.5 cm x 26.5 cm)

SHOPPING LIST

Yarn (Medium Weight) MEDIUM 4
[4 ounces, 235 yards
(113 grams, 215 meters) per
skein]:
☐ Color A (Yellow) - 2 skeins
☐ Color B (Blue) - 1 skein
☐ Color C (Green) - 1 skein

Crochet Hook
☐ Size I (5.5 mm)
or size needed for gauge

GAUGE INFORMATION

Holding 2 strands together,
11 hdc and 8 rows/rnds = 4"
(10 cm)

Gauge Swatch: 4" (10 cm) square
Holding 2 strands of Color A together, ch 13.

Row 1: Hdc in third ch from hook and in each ch across: 11 hdc.

Rows 2-8: Ch 2 **(beginning ch-2 does not count as a st)**, turn; hdc in first hdc and in each hdc across. Finish off.

INSTRUCTIONS

Basket is worked holding two strands of yarn together throughout.

BOTTOM

Rnd 1: Holding 2 strands of Color A together, make an adjustable loop to form a ring *(Figs. 1a-d, page 45)*, ch 2 **(beginning ch-2 does not count as a st, now and throughout)**, work 10 hdc in ring; join with slip st to top of beginning ch-2.

Rnd 2: Ch 2, 2 hdc in each hdc around; join with slip st to top of beginning ch-2: 20 hdc.

Rnd 3: Ch 2, hdc in first hdc, 2 hdc in next hdc, (hdc in next hdc, 2 hdc in next hdc) around; join with slip st to top of beginning ch-2: 30 hdc.

Rnd 4: Ch 2, hdc in first 2 hdc, 2 hdc in next hdc, (hdc in next 2 hdc, 2 hdc in next hdc) around; join with slip st to top of beginning ch-2: 40 hdc.

Rnd 5: Ch 2, hdc in first 3 hdc, 2 hdc in next hdc, (hdc in next 3 hdc, 2 hdc in next hdc) around; join with slip st to top of beginning ch-2: 50 hdc.

Rnd 6: Ch 2, hdc in first 4 hdc, 2 hdc in next hdc, (hdc in next 4 hdc, 2 hdc in next hdc) around; join with slip st to top of beginning ch-2: 60 hdc.

Rnd 7: Ch 2, hdc in first 5 hdc, 2 hdc in next hdc, (hdc in next 5 hdc, 2 hdc in next hdc) around; join with slip st to top of beginning ch-2: 70 hdc.

Rnd 8: Ch 2, hdc in first 6 hdc, 2 hdc in next hdc, (hdc in next 6 hdc, 2 hdc in next hdc) around; join with slip st to top of beginning ch-2: 80 hdc.

Rnd 9: Ch 2, hdc in first 7 hdc, 2 hdc in next hdc, (hdc in next 7 hdc, 2 hdc in next hdc) around; join with slip st to top of beginning ch-2: 90 hdc.

Rnd 10: Ch 2, hdc in first 8 hdc, 2 hdc in next hdc, (hdc in next 8 hdc, 2 hdc in next hdc) around; join with slip st to top of beginning ch-2: 100 hdc.

SIDES

Rnd 1 (Right side)**:** Ch 2, working in Back Loops Only ***(Fig. 3, page 46)***, sc in first hdc, dc in next hdc, (sc in next hdc, dc in next hdc) around; join with slip st to top of beginning ch-2.

Rnd 2: Ch 2, **turn**; working in both loops, sc in first dc, dc in next sc, (sc in next dc, dc in next sc) around; join with slip st to top of beginning ch-2.

Rnds 3 and 4: Repeat Rnd 2.

Rnd 5: Ch 2, turn; sc in first dc, dc in next sc, (sc in next dc, dc in next sc) around; cut one strand, holding remaining strand and 1 strand of Color B together, join with slip st to top of beginning ch-2 ***(Fig. 6b, page 46)***.

Repeat Rnd 2 for pattern, working in the following Stripe Sequence: 4 Rnds holding 1 strand of Color A & 1 strand of Color B, 5 rnds holding 2 strands of Color B, 4 rnds holding 1 strand of Color B & 1 strand of Color C, 1 rnd holding 2 strands of Color C; do **not** finish off.

HANDLES

Rnd 1: With Color C, ch 2, turn; sc in first dc, dc in next sc, (sc in next dc, dc in next sc) 7 times, ch 15, skip next 15 sts, dc in next sc, (sc in next dc, dc in next sc) 17 times, ch 15, skip next 15 sts, dc in next sc, (sc in next dc, dc in next sc) around; join with slip st to top of beginning ch-2: 70 sts and 30 chs.

Rnds 2-5: Ch 2, turn; sc in first dc, dc in next sc, (sc in next st, dc in next st) around; join with slip st to top of beginning ch-2: 100 sts.

Finish off.

Design by Marly Bird.

GENERAL INSTRUCTIONS

ABBREVIATIONS

BPsc	Back Post single crochet(s)
ch	chain(s)
cm	centimeters
dc	double crochet(s)
dc2tog	double crochet 2 together
ex sc	extended single crochet(s)
hdc	half double crochet(s)
hdc2tog	half double crochet 2 together
mm	millimeters
Rnd(s)	Round(s)
sc	single crochet(s)
sc2tog	single crochet 2 together
sp(s)	space(s)
st(s)	stitch(es)
YO	yarn over

SYMBOLS & TERMS

★ — work instructions following ★ as many **more** times as indicated in addition to the first time.

( ) or **[ ]** — work enclosed instructions **as many** times as specified by the number immediately following **or** work all enclosed instructions in the stitch or space indicated **or** contains explanatory remarks.

colon (:) — the number(s) given after a colon at the end of a row or round denote(s) the number ofstitches or spaces you should have on that row or round.

CROCHET TERMINOLOGY		
UNITED STATES		INTERNATIONAL
slip stitch (slip st)	=	single crochet (sc)
single crochet (sc)	=	double crochet (dc)
half double crochet (hdc)	=	half treble crochet (htr)
double crochet (dc)	=	treble crochet (tr)
treble crochet (tr)	=	double treble crochet (dtr)
double treble crochet (dtr)	=	triple treble crochet (ttr)
triple treble crochet (tr tr)	=	quadruple treble crochet (qtr)
skip	=	miss

GAUGE

Exact gauge is **essential** for proper size. Before beginning your project, make the sample swatch given in the individual instructions in the yarn and hook specified. After completing the swatch, measure it, counting your stitches and rows or rounds carefully. If your swatch is larger or smaller than specified, **make another, changing hook size to get the correct gauge**. Keep trying until you find the size hook that will give you the specified gauge.

Yarn Weight Symbol & Names	LACE 0	SUPER FINE 1	FINE 2	LIGHT 3	MEDIUM 4	BULKY 5	SUPER BULKY 6	JUMBO 7
Type of Yarns in Category	Fingering, size 10 crochet thread	Sock, Fingering, Baby	Sport, Baby	DK, Light Worsted	Worsted, Afghan, Aran	Chunky, Craft, Rug	Super Bulky, Roving	Jumbo, Roving
Crochet Gauge* Ranges in Single Crochet to 4" (10 cm)	32-42 sts**	21-32 sts	16-20 sts	12-17 sts	11-14 sts	8-11 sts	6-9 sts	5 sts and fewer
Advised Hook Size Range	Steel*** 6 to 8, Regular hook B-1	B-1 to E-4	E-4 to 7	7 to I-9	I-9 to K-10½	K-10½ to M/N-13	M/N-13 to Q	Q and larger

*GUIDELINES ONLY: The chart above reflects the most commonly used gauges and hook sizes for specific yarn categories.

** Lace weight yarns are usually crocheted with larger hooks to create lacy openwork patterns. Accordingly, a gauge range is difficult to determine. Always follow the gauge stated in your pattern.

*** Steel crochet hooks are sized differently from regular hooks–the higher the number, the smaller the hook, which is the reverse of regular hook sizing.

CROCHET HOOKS																	
U.S.	B-1	C-2	D-3	E-4	F-5	G-6	7	H-8	I-9	J-10	K-10½	L-11	M/N-13	N/P-15	P/Q	Q	S
Metric - mm	2.25	2.75	3.25	3.5	3.75	4	4.5	5	5.5	6	6.5	8	9	10	15	16	19

BEGINNER	Projects for first-time crocheters using basic stitches. Minimal shaping.
EASY	Projects using yarn with basic stitches, repetitive stitch patterns, simple color changes, and simple shaping and finishing.
INTERMEDIATE	Projects using a variety of techniques, such as basic lace patterns or color patterns, mid-level shaping and finishing.
EXPERIENCED	Projects with intricate stitch patterns, techniques and dimension, such as non-repeating patterns, multi-color techniques, fine threads, small hooks, detailed shaping and refined finishing.

MARKERS

Markers are used to help distinguish the beginning of each round being worked. Place a 2" (5 cm) scrap piece of yarn before the first stitch of each round, moving marker after each round is complete.

JOINING WITH SC

When instructed to join with sc, begin with a slip knot on hook. Insert hook in stitch or space indicated, YO and pull up a loop, YO and draw through both loops on hook.

ADJUSTABLE LOOP

Wind yarn around two fingers to form a ring ***(Fig. 1a)***. Slide yarn off fingers and grasp the strands at the top of the ring ***(Fig. 1b)***. Insert hook from **front** to **back** into the ring, pull up a loop, YO and draw through loop on hook to lock ring ***(Fig. 1c)*** **(st made does not count as a beginning ch)**. Working around both strands, follow instructions to work sts in the ring, then pull yarn tail to close ***(Fig. 1d)***.

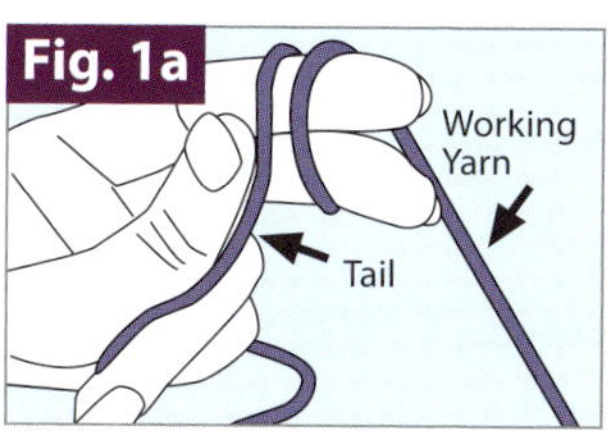

Fig. 1a

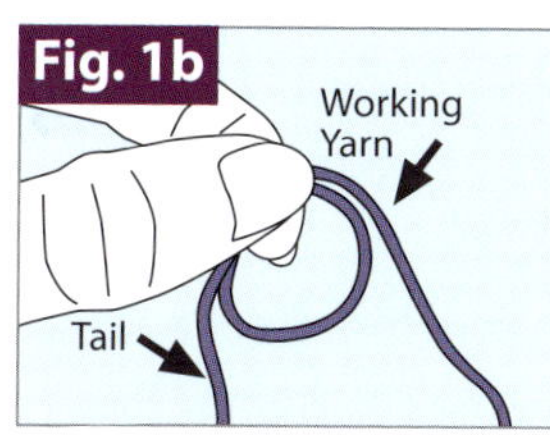

Fig. 1b

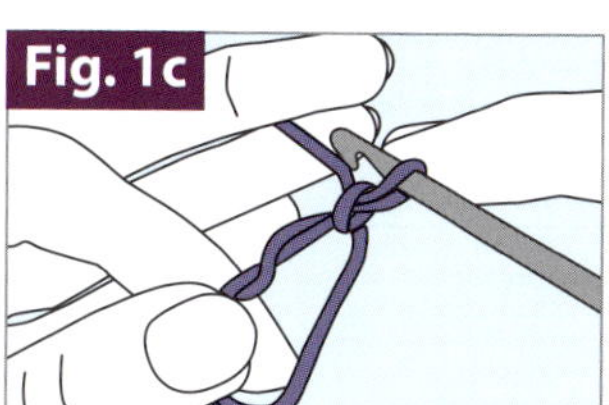
Fig. 1c

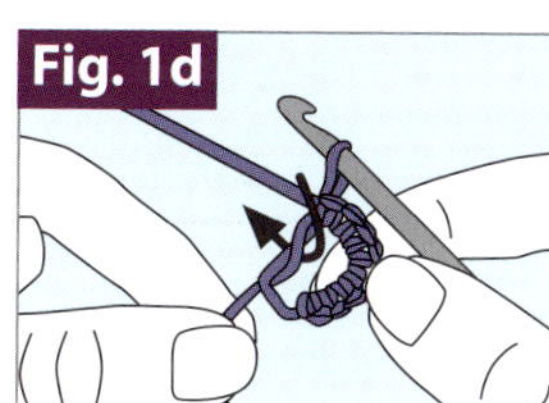
Fig. 1d

BACK RIDGE

Work only in loop(s) indicated by arrow *(Fig. 2)*.

Fig. 2

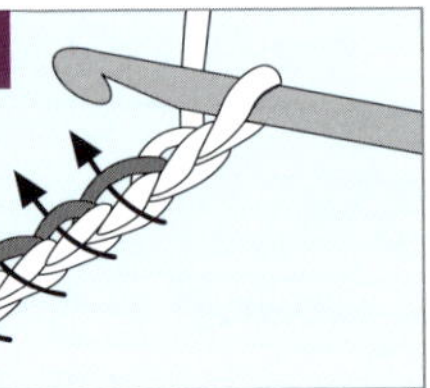

BACK LOOP ONLY

Work only in loop(s) indicated by arrow *(Fig. 3)*.

Fig. 3

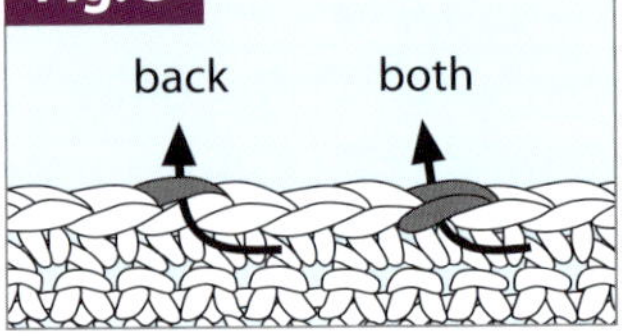

WORKING IN FRONT OF OR BEHIND A STITCH

Work in stitch or space indicated, inserting hook in direction of arrow *(Fig. 4)*.

Fig. 4

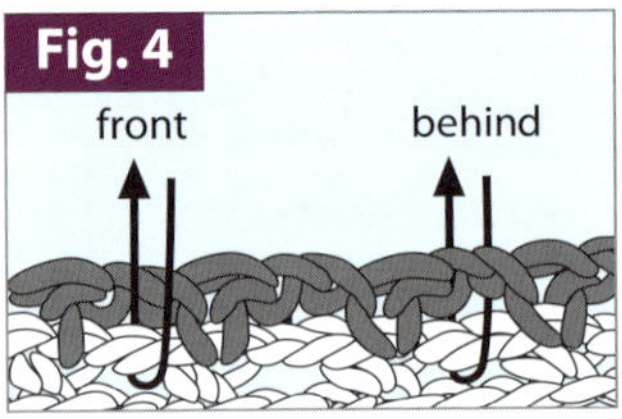

FREE LOOPS OF CHAIN

When instructed to work in free loops of a beginning chain, work in loop indicated by arrow *(Fig. 5)*.

Fig. 5

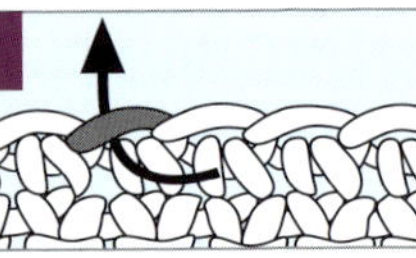

CHANGING COLORS

To change colors in last stitch made, work the last stitch to within one step of completion, drop or cut yarn as specified, hook new yarn *(Fig. 6a)* and draw through all loops on hook.

Fig. 6a

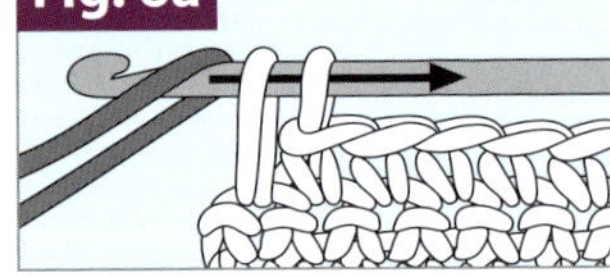

To change colors with slip st, drop yarn to **wrong** side, insert hook in stitch indicated, hook new yarn and draw through stitch and loop on hook *(Fig. 6b)*.

Fig. 6b

WHIPSTITCH

With the **right** side together and edges even, sew through both sides once to secure the seam, leaving an ample yarn end to weave in later. Insert the needle from **back** to **front** through two strands on each piece *(Figs. 7a & b)*.

Fig. 7a

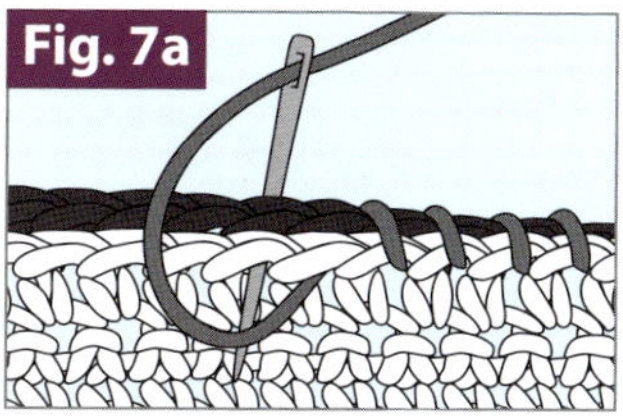

Fig. 7b

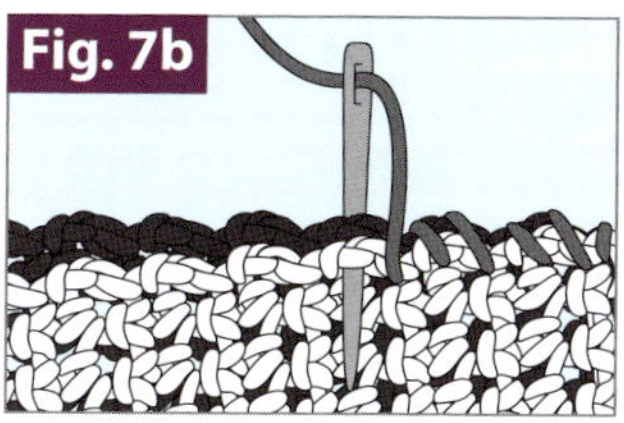

Bring the needle around and insert it from **back** to **front** through the next strands on both pieces. Continue in this manner, drawing seam together as you work.

WEAVE THRU STITCHES

Thread yarn needle with long end and weave it through the stitches on the last round *(Fig. 8)*.

Fig. 8

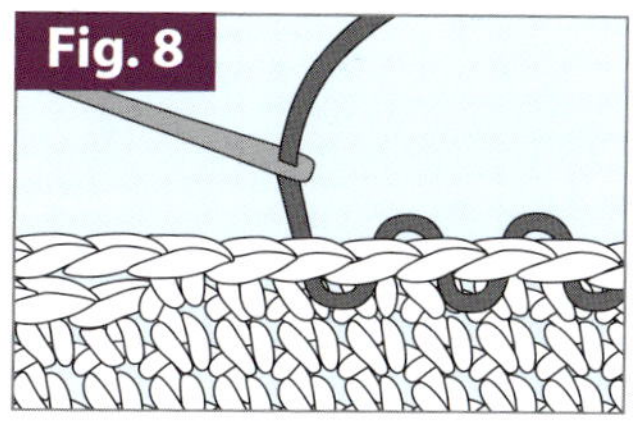

We have made every effort to ensure that these instructions are accurate and complete. We cannot, however, be responsible for human error, typographical mistakes, or variations in individual work.

Instructions tested and photo models made by Janet Akins, Marianna Crowder, Lee Ellis, and Raymelle Greening.

Production Team: Writer/Technical Editor - Cathy Hardy; Editorial Writer - Susan Frantz Wiles; Senior Graphic Artist - Lora Puls; Graphic Artist - Cailen Cochran; Photo Stylist - Lori Wenger; and Photographer - Jason Masters.

YARN INFORMATIION

The items in this book were made using Caron United, a Medium Weight yarn. Any brand of medium weight yarn may be used. It is best to refer to the yardage/meters when determining how many skeins or balls to purchase. Remember, to arrive at the finished size, it is the GAUGE/TENSION that is important, not the brand of yarn.

For your convenience, listed below are the colors used to create our photography models. Because yarn manufacturers make frequent changes in their product lines, you may sometimes find it necessary to use a substitute yarn or to search for the discontinued product at alternate suppliers (locally or online).

MARY JANE SLIPPERS
Main Color - #06015 Orchid
Contrasting Color - #06002 Aran

FAMILY CUFFED SLIPPERS
#06003 Mocha

BABY BOOTIES & MITTS
Color A - #06017 Light Blue
Color B - #06001 White

FAMILY HAT
Red & Blue Model
Main Color - #06007 Cherry
Contrasting Color - #06013 Royal
Grey Model
Main Color - #06005 Dark Grey Heather
Contrasting Color - #06004 Soft Grey Heather

FAMILY NECKWEAR
Solid Scarf
#06005 Dark Grey Heather
2-Color Scarf
Main Color - #06007 Cherry
Contrasting Color - #06013 Royal
Hooded Scarf
Main Color - #06008 Red
Contrasting Color - #06005 Dark Grey Heather
Cowl
#06009 Burgundy

LACY MITTS
2-Color Mitts
Main Color - #06006 Black
Contrasting Color - #06002 Aran
5-Color Mitts
Main Color - #06012 Fresh Green
Color A - #06008 Red
Color B - #06010 Orange
Color C - #06011 Mustard
Color D - #06001 White

BASIC MITTS
#06004 Soft Grey Heather

PET BED
Main Color - #06014 Navy
Contrasting Color - #06004 Soft Grey Heather

BARGELLO COVER-UPS
Car Seat Cover
Color A - #06001 White
Color B - #06012 Fresh Green
Color C - #06016 Dark Green
Lap Robe
Color A - #06005 Dark Grey Heather
Color B - #06011 Mustard
Color C - #06012 Fresh Green

BASKET
Color A - #06011 Mustard
Color B - #06017 Light Blue
Color C - #06012 Fresh Green